Young Learner's

Step by Step

Young Learner Publications®

G-1A Rattan Jyoti, 18 Rajendra Place, New Delhi- 110 008 (INDIA)
Tel: 25750801, 25820556, 25755559 Fax: 91-11-25764396
Website: www.goodwillpublishinghouse.com
E-mail: gph.ylp@goodwillpublishinghouse.com
goodwillpub@gmail.com

Basic Shading Techniques

Pencil shading plays a very important role in drawing still life, landscape and portrait, etc. You can see how a two-dimensional drawing converts into three-dimensional form simply by using pencil tones. An important point to keep in mind before starting the work is to always use one technique for one subject and not to mix two or more techniques. Start with light shading and proceed to dark shading. Do not press the pencil too hard while shading as it kills the grains of the paper. Carefully, see the direction of strokes of each technique and apply on the paper.

Observe the different techniques of pencil-shading strokes below. Copy the pencil-shading techniques in the blank boxes given alongside using a 2B lead pencil. Besides this exercise practise these pencil-shading techniques in your sketchbook also.

Hatching	Cross-hatching	Hatching	Cross-hatching
Curved lines	Curved cross-hatching	Curved lines	Curved cross-hatching
Scribbling	Soft blending	Scribbling	Soft blending

In this lesson we shall learn drawing and shading by hatching technique that has been used to create the still-life object given below with a 2B pencil on cartridge paper. Carefully read each step to understand how to create 3D effect in a 2D drawing by using shading tones. Apply this method on all pencil-shading techniques.

Original pot

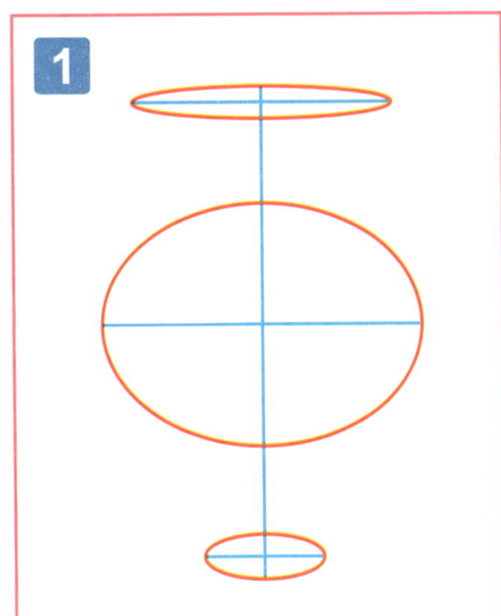

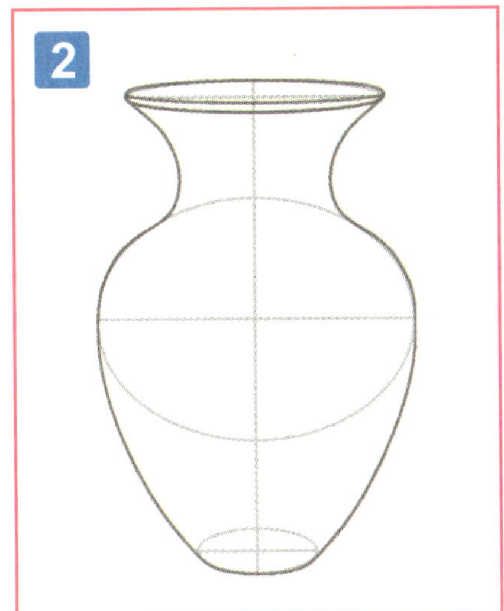

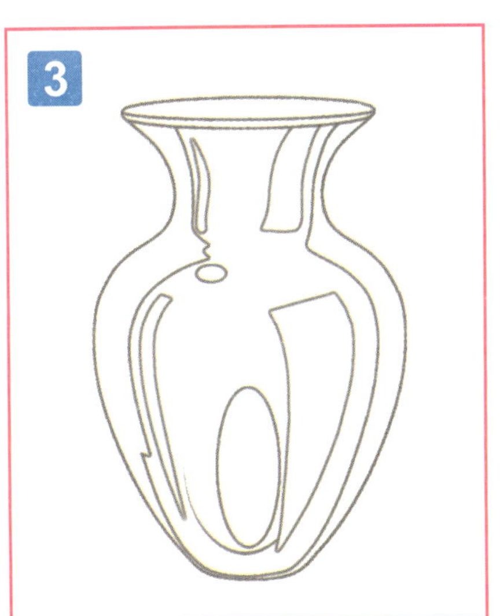

1. Observe the original pot carefully. Draw the basic pot shape and proportions using wire frame forms.
2. Sketch the outer shape of the pot.
3. Now, lightly sketch and divide the various tones like highlights, middle tones, dark shadows and reflections. Erase the lines of transparent wire frame.
4. Starting from dark part, lightly apply some basic strokes. Make sure that all shading strokes are in one single direction.
5. Add more middle and dark shading tones without pressing the pencil. Do not rub the pencil on the paper, instead add more strokes to make dark shades.
6. Finally, add more pencil strokes to the final details. The pot drawing is now ready.

You can try drawing other objects using this technique.

Drawing a Still Life

Still-life objects around us might seem ordinary. These objects can be natural, man-made or both. But, if you arrange these objects together in a particular manner, the seemingly ordinary collection of objects transforms into an extraordinary still-life composition. In this exercise, we shall start with very basic shapes and objects to draw a still-life composition. You only require a 2B pencil, eraser and an A3 cartridge paper. Let's start!

Carefully read and follow all the steps to learn to place and draw a still-life composition.

The first step to make a still-life composition is to select and arrange the different objects in an interesting manner. We have to collect simple everyday objects of different shapes, sizes and colours and then arrange them. Overlapping of the objects plays a very important part and should be done carefully. Lighting is also an important element of a still-life composition. Beginners should try to arrange the objects in a room where artificial light comes from the side. A 45° angle from yourself is the most commonly used angle for composing a still life. Light which comes from the back and the front flattens the subject.

Once you are satisfied with the shape, proportion and composition of the still life, draw the outlines of the objects in a transparent wire frame form with visible lines of construction. Remember, while drawing the objects compare the shape of the objects with each other in order to get the right proportion. Also, check the position of whole composition on the sheet. Draw lines with a very light pencil as this makes it easier to correct any mistakes and erase the lines of construction.

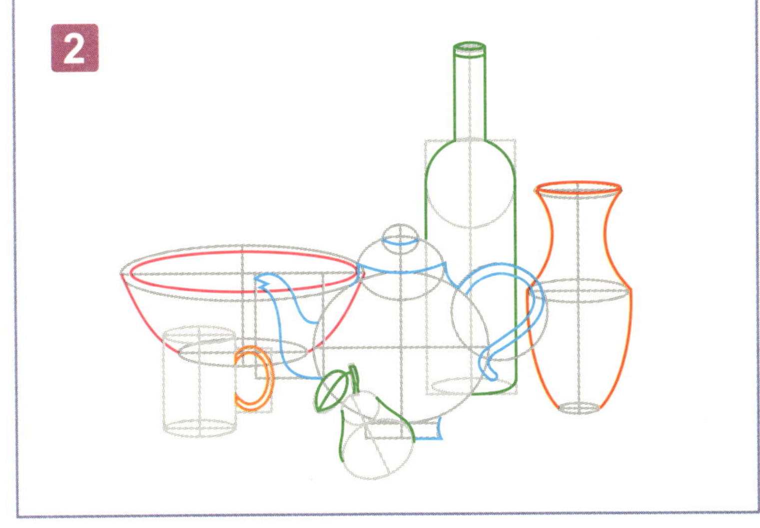

2. After completing the objects draw outer and inner details of each object with a light pencil (see the coloured lines in step 2).

3. Now, erase the lines of construction. This will leave you with clean visible outlines of each object (as shown in step 3). Now, your still life is ready for pencil shading.

4. Before you start shading, observe the whole composition carefully. Make a note of the lightest and the darkest objects. Remember to keep a piece of paper under your hand so that the work does not get smudged. Always shade from light to dark. First, apply some basic light tones to each object. Divide each object into light, middle and dark tones. This will help you to build up its three-dimensional form. We will not highlight any part of the object while shading. Do not complete any object in one go, but apply shading on the entire composition step by step.

After completing the still life, fix the work with the help of a fixative. Make sure that you take the help of an elder person while using the spray. Let the composition dry completely before framing it.

For teachers and parents: Encourage the children to collect several objects like book, ball, shoe box, bottle, pot, crockery, etc. Arrange the objects into an interesting composition. They should practise different angles of still life in their sketchbooks.

Drawing Drapery Folds

Drapery is a very important part of the still-life background or base. It enhances the form of objects and increases the impact of the image. Drapery is a piece of fabric, especially as arranged in loose, graceful folds, which hang from one, two or more points of support as per requirement of the still life. All folds come from these points. Each fold links with the other like a puzzle. In this exercise we shall learn about different types of folds. We shall draw drapery without and with still-life compositions. We shall be able to draw clothing of all types once we learn the art of drapery drawing.

Carefully observe the different types of basic drapery folds explained below. Practice these drapery folds in your sketchbook using a 2B lead pencil.

1 Pipe folds

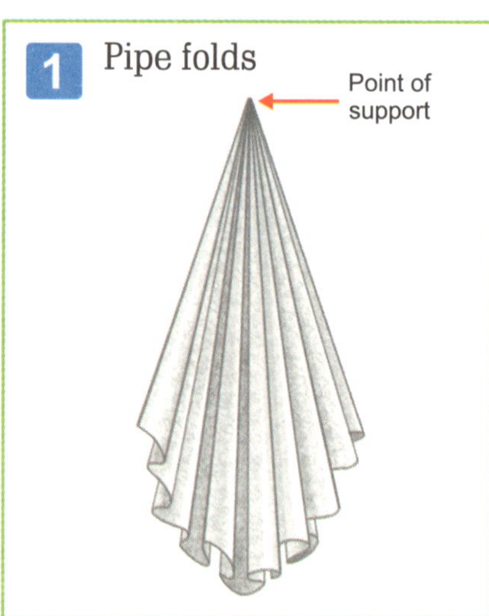

2 Diaper folds

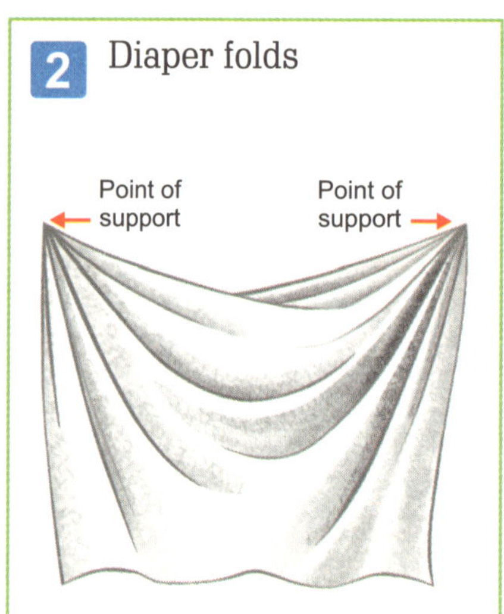

3 Zigzag folds

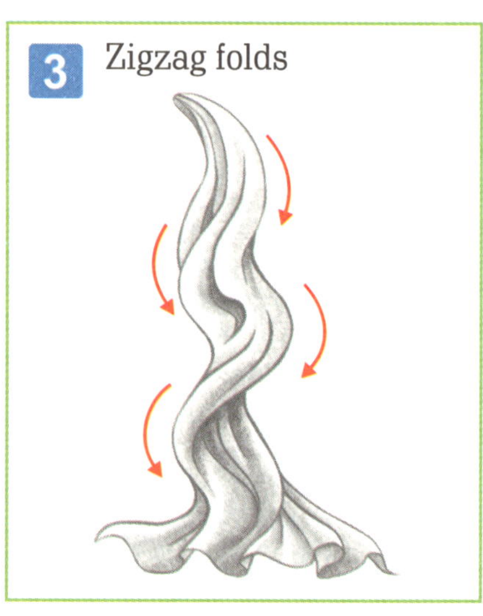

4 Half-lock folds

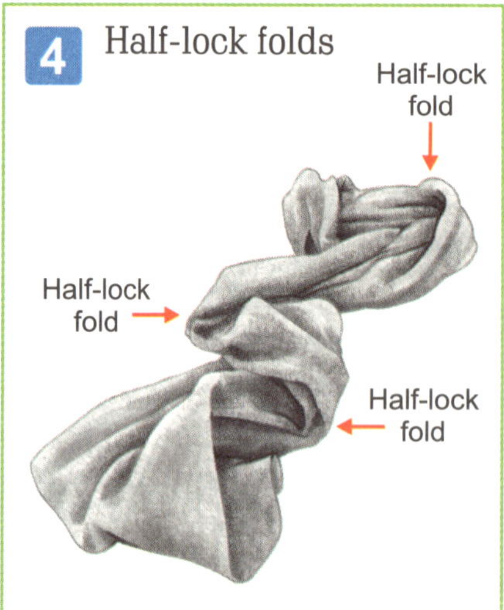

1. **Pipe folds** - These folds are made when the drapery does not touch the ground. The lower part of the folds are rounded and cylindrical in shape.
2. **Diaper folds** - These folds have two points of support. The top of the curve is usually sharp, and the lower side of the fold is softly shaded. The angle of the folds and curves will change if you shift the position of the points of support.
3. **Zigzag folds** - If you twist the pipe folds and the drapery touches the ground, the zigzag will be on the slack side of the bend. Each slack section folds in contrast to the next one, interlocking zigzag. These zigzags may not be even.
4. **Half-lock fold** - The half-lock always occurs as the result of change in direction of the piece of cloth. The focus is on the point where the direction changes. This fold always occurs on the slack side.

5 Spiral folds

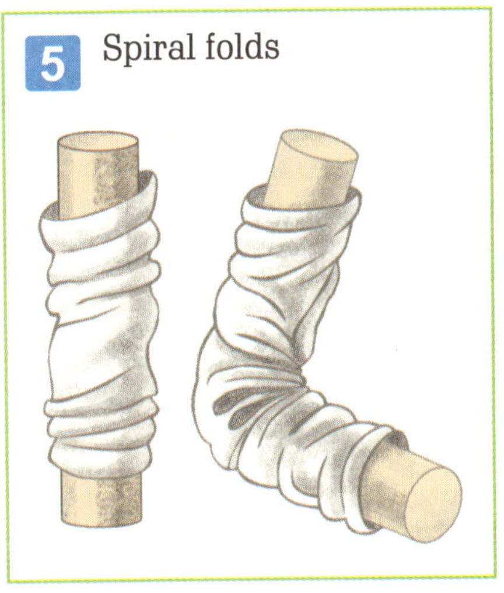

6 Inert folds

5. **Spiral folds** - These folds appear in a tubular form. Spiral folds follow the form and change their angle where the form changes its direction.
6. **Inert folds** - Inert folds usually contain a mix variety of folds. All the folds appear like a group of irregular ridges, resting on a flat surface. Inert folds change along with the shape of the surface on which they are resting.

Carefully read and observe the steps given below to understand how to draw a drapery with folds.

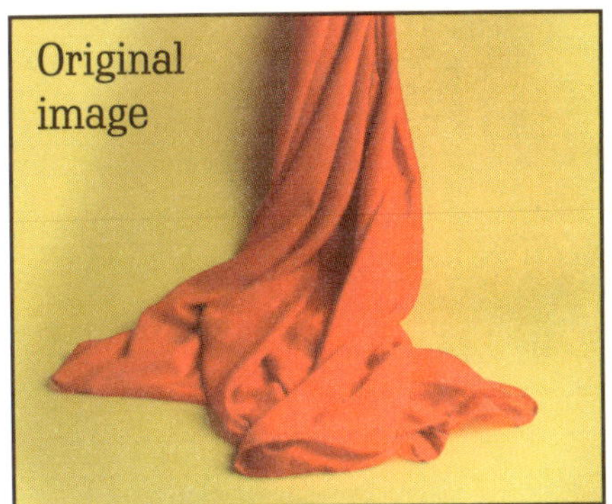

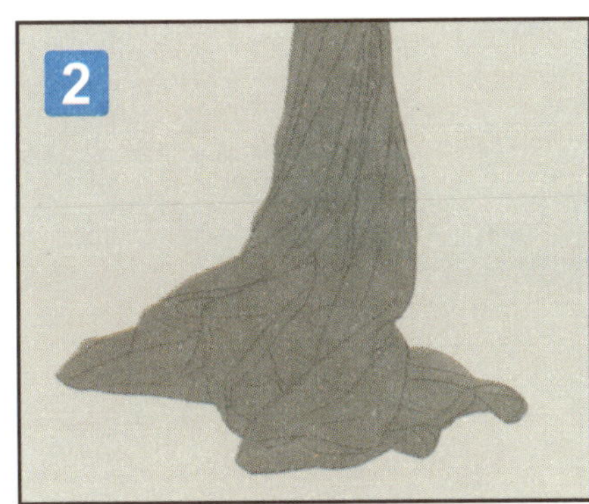

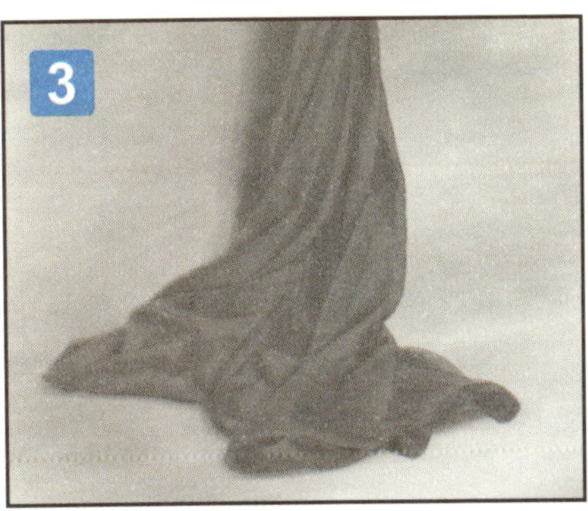

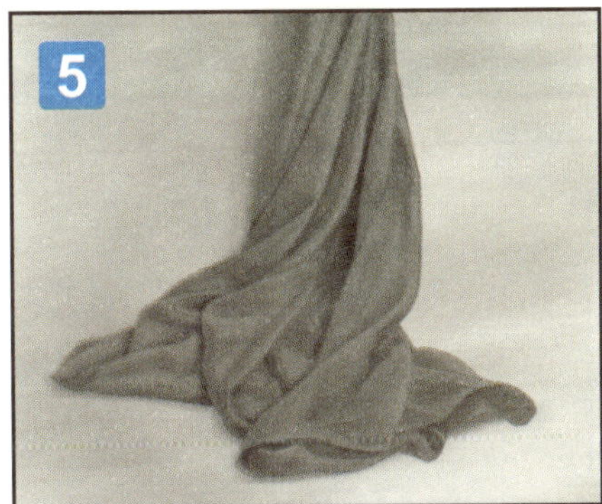

Looking at the outer shape of the drapery, first draw light outlines with a 2B pencil. Observe the original image and convert coloured tones into black and white tones. Fill a light tone with the pencil into drapery outline (see figure 2). Then, fill middle and dark tones to make the folds (see figures 3 and 4). Finally, fill in the dark tones (see figure 5). Do not press the pencil too hard.

In this exercise we shall learn how to draw and shade a still-life object by hatching technique. We shall use colour pencils on a cartridge paper. First, we shall draw the outlines of still life with a very light pencil (see figure 1). Fill in very light tones in each object and drapery (see figure 2). Then, fill the second tone in each object to make a three-dimensional form (see figure 3). Now, fill the middle and dark tones (see figure 4). Finally, compare the still life with original image and give the final touches to objects, drapery and background (see figure 5).

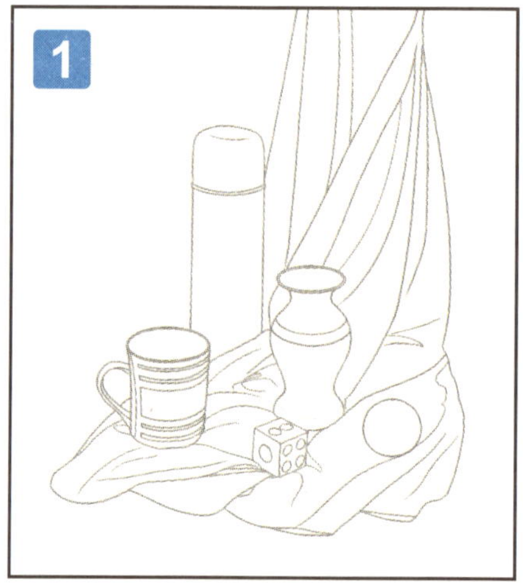

In this lesson we shall draw and shade a composition of a pot and flowers using colour pencils on cartridge paper. In natural objects like flowers, trees and leaves it is very difficult to measure the proportion of objects. The simplest way to draw in the right proportion is by carefully observing the whole bunch of flowers, and drawing an outer form with a very light pencil. Then, draw individual flowers and leaves (see figure 1). Now, fill very light tones in each outline (see figure 2). Next, fill second tones in each object to separate the objects (see figure 3). Finally, give final touches to the dark parts of the petals and leaves (see figure 4).

1

2

3

4

Study the still life given below.
It has been drawn using pencil colours. Follow the same step-by-step technique mentioned on previous page to draw this composition. If you compare the draperies used on this page and page 8, you will notice an overall difference between the two draperies. This is because we have used cotton drapery on page 8 and a satin drapery for this still life. Both the fabrics are different from each other as the satin cloth is shinier than the cotton cloth.

Carefully observe the still life given on the previous page. You have to copy the colours and shading in the drawing given below using colour pencils.

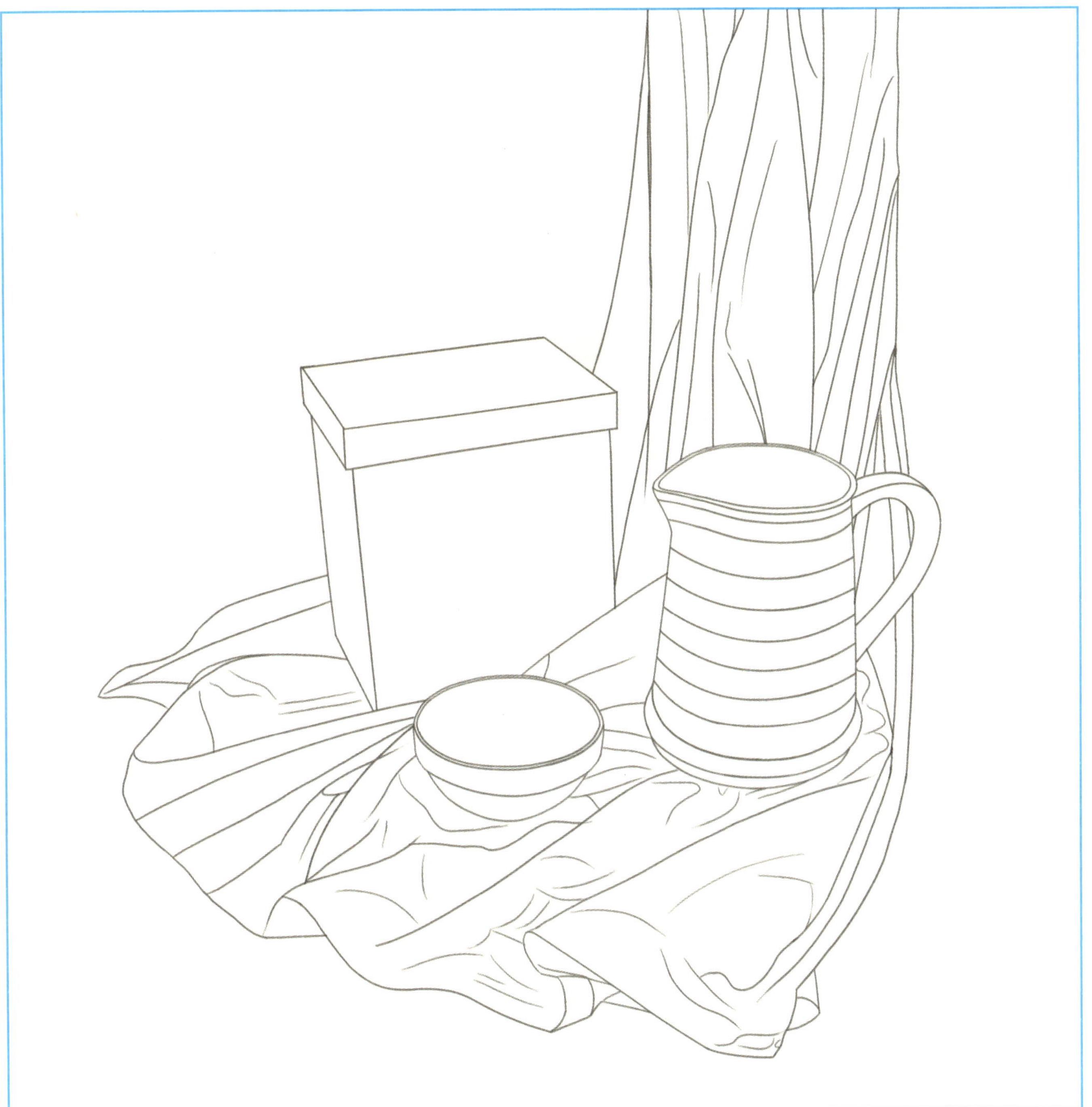

For teachers and parents: Besides this exercise, encourage the children to practise more still-life compositions by using objects of different shapes, colours and made of different materials like wood, glass, plastic, etc. The children can also use fruits, flowers and leaves and make interesting still-life compositions in their sketchbooks.

For draperies, experiment with different types of fabrics and folds by changing the position of the points of support. The selection of the drapery colour depends on the colour of the objects being used in the still life. Always start practising with lead pencil and later, you can use colour pencils.

Places We Visit

In this exercise, we will practice drawing different places like garden, metro station, market, beach and a water park. In all these places we shall be drawing human figures too. Refer to the human sketches you have drawn before. Choose the sketches that are appropriate for the chosen place. For example, to draw metro-station scene, you can select standing and sitting poses of men, women and kids. Add some bags or briefcases in their hands and place the figures on the station according to the size and perspective. There is no need to physically visit each place to draw it. You can refer to magazines and photographs for ideas to draw the compositions.

Carefully observe the picnic scene below. The important part of this scene is that all family members are sitting together and bonding with each other. Also, notice the arrangement of things like fruit basket, plates, jug, ball, etc. The first step is to draw a light sketch and to fill a light tone in each shape. Next, work on the background and then on the human figures and other objects.

Carefully observe the metro-station scene given below based on one-point perspective. Colour the same scene in the box given below with colour pencils. Follow the step-by-step colour and shading techniques as shown on previous pages.

Carefully observe the market scene given below based on one-point perspective. Colour the same scene in the box given below using colour pencils.

Carefully observe the beach scene given below. Colour the same scene in the box given below using colour pencils.

For teachers and parents: Encourage the children to practise drawing different beach scenes by using travel magazines as reference.

Carefully observe the water-park scene given below. Colour the same scene in the box given below with colour pencils.

For teachers and parents: Encourage the children to practise drawing different places using observations from daily life, photographs and travel magazines as reference.